"Talk Your Way to Success: Unveiling the Secrets of Effective Communication"

Willard T. Lewis

Table of Contents

INTRODUCTION

In the bustling heart of a sprawling metropolis, where the city's regenerative energy could easily overwhelm even the most outgoing souls, there lived a man named Willard T. Lewis. In the grand tapestry of life, he was what some might call an unlikely protagonist. Willard, you see, had spent a significant portion of his life navigating the intricate labyrinth of small talk and social interactions.

In a world that often praised grand speeches and dazzling presentations, Willard's true mastery lay in the subtle art of conversation. He possessed a skill that some might dismiss as insignificant—the ability to engage in causal conversation with grace and finesse. Yet, beneath the surface of these seemingly casual exchanges lay a depth of understanding and empathy that set him apart.

Willard was not a charismatic extrovert who effortlessly commanded attention in a room. Instead, he was a quiet observer, an attentive listener, and a skilled conversationalist who knew the secrets to forging connections and leaving a lasting positive impression.

As you turn the pages of this book, you'll embark on a remarkable journey alongside Willard T. Lewis. Together, you'll explore the transformative power of causal conversation—an art that can elevate ordinary interactions into meaningful connections, shape the trajectory of careers, and enrich the tapestry of human relationships.

In the chapters that follow, you'll discover the hidden wisdom of a man who understood that sometimes, it's the smallest conversations that can lead to the most significant transformations. Whether you seek to enhance your professional network, strengthen personal relationships, or simply navigate life's social intricacies with finesse, Willard's insights and experiences will guide you toward mastering the art of conversation and social grace.

So, dear reader, as you step into Willard's world and embark on this journey, prepare to unlock the secrets of social grace, discover the beauty of causal conversation, and witness the remarkable transformation that can occur when you embrace the power of meaningful connections.

CHAPTER 1

THE POWER OF EFFECTIVE COMMUNICATION

What is effective communication?

Effective communication is the process of exchanging ideas, thoughts, opinions, knowledge, and data so that the message is received and understood with clarity and purpose. When we communicate effectively, both the sender and receiver feel satisfied.

We spend our time communicating. In fact, we can't get enough of it – so much so that we have found new and inventive ways to do it. However, while our means of communication may evolve and multiply, the essence of effective communication remains unchanged. Whether it be in the interview room or at the negotiation table, effective communication is often the difference between good and great.

So what is it exactly and what tools can get us there?

THE POWER OF GOOD COMMUNICATION

Imagine the situation: An important presentation to investors. Months of work behind it. You have the soft skills. You know the business. You have analysed the case. And now all that is left to do is to present and defend your proposal.

In this and every other situation, effective communication comes to the fore. In the heat of the moment, it is the gestures we choose and the language we use that decide the outcome. There is sometimes a very thin line between failure and success and effective communication can often determine which side of the line we find ourselves.

How to communicate effectively

There is a path for every one of us to improve how we communicate. In one situation, we can achieve almost effortless communication while in another we will be lost for words and painstakingly deliberating over the best way to get our ideas and intentions across.

So how do we think we might make a challenging situation as accessible as a chat with a friend?

- **Build awareness and understanding**

In order to communicate effectively, we must call on our powers of awareness. Here lies the difference between talking and communicating.

- **Self-awareness**

Asking ourselves how we want to be perceived and what our goals are is a great starting point for building effective communication. With this knowledge, we can be surprised with the feedback others can offer.

- **Situational Understanding**

Who am I speaking with? What is their world view? What is the context? What signals am I receiving? We can look to understand the other person's viewpoint and adapt our communication accordingly.

Build trust, create clarity

- **Bridge-Building**

Communication is not a two-way street. It is a bridge. And if you don't have one, you need to build one. While conflict is natural and inevitable at times, effective communication always looks to build trust and collaboration to create new pathways for interaction. As difficult as a situation might be, communication always matters. Even in the most trying moments, opportunities to build trust abound! "Even if I have disappointing results, how I communicate those results still makes a difference. There will be a next time".

- **Matching Words to Intention**

By asking yourself the right questions, clearly communicating your intent with words that match your intention will follow naturally. Aligning intent and communication is the key to powerful and effective communication.

Just imagine a world of clear, effective communicators!

Exposure to an international and challenging environment is the ideal practise ground to learn this vital skill. Effective communication is the key tool that allows you to get your point across and to persuade your listener to act on what you are saying. And whatever the situation, it is the trusty tool to help you achieve your objectives!

WHY EFFECTIVE COMMUNICATION MATTERS

Communication is a vital aspect of our daily lives. It allows us to express our thoughts, ideas, and emotions to others and to understand the perspectives of others in return.

Communication occurs in many forms, including verbal and non-verbal, written, visual, and listening. It can occur in person, on the internet (on forums, social media, and websites), over the phone (through apps, calls, and video), or by mail.

For communication to be effective, it must be CLEAR, CORRECT, COMPLETE, CONCISE, and COMPASSIONATE. We consider these to be 5 C's of communication, though they may vary depending on who you're asking.

While the effectiveness of communication can be difficult to measure, its impact is hard to deny. According to one study, surveyed companies in the United States and United Kingdom with at least 100, 000 employees lost $62. 4 million per year on average due to poor communication. On the flip side, companies led by effective communicators had nearly 50 percent higher total returns to shareholders over companies with less effective communicators at the helm.

Effective communication is especially important when trying to build trust.

Benefits of Effective Communication

The benefits of communication effectiveness can be witnessed in the workplace, in an educational setting, and in your personal life. Learning how to communicate well can be a boon in each of these areas.

- **Trust is the foundation of all strong relationships, whether they be personal or professional.**

Trust enables us to feel secure in our interactions with others, knowing they will be honest and reliable in their actions and words. Good communication plays a key role in building and maintaining trust. When we communicate openly, clearly, and respectfully, we signal to others that we value their opinions and are committed to being transparent in our dealings with them.

- **Poor communication can quickly erode trust and damage relationships.**

Miscommunication can lead to misunderstandings and misinterpretations, which can result in hurt feelings, frustration, and resentment. In order to build strong relationships, it is important to make a conscious effort to communicate effectively, by being clear and concise in our messages, actively listening to others, and being open to feedback and constructive criticism.

- **In professional settings, strong communication skills are particularly valuable.**

Great communication helps to build rapport with colleagues, negotiate conflicts, and work towards common goals. In the workplace, trust is particularly important, as it is essential for team members to be able to rely on one another to fulfill their responsibilities and meet deadlines. Good communication can help build trust between team members, enabling them to work together more effectively and efficiently.

Communication is a crucial aspect of building and maintaining trust and relationships.

Whether we are interacting with friends, family, or colleagues, effective communication skills are essential for fostering positive, productive, and fulfilling relationships. By making a conscious effort to communicate effectively, we can build trust, improve our relationships, and ultimately achieve our goals and aspirations.

In your personal life, effective communication can lead to:

- Improved social, emotional, and mental health
- Deeper existing connections
- New bonds based on trust and transparency
- Better problem–solving and conflict resolution skills

In the workplace, effective communication can help you:

- Manage employees and build teams
- Grow your organization more rapidly and retain employees
- Benefit from enhanced creativity and innovation.
- Build strong relationships and attract more opportunities for you or your organization

THE IMPACT OF SOCIAL GRACE

Social graces are skills used to interact in social situations. They include manners, etiquette (the specifically accepted ques within a culture for the application of universal manners) department, fashion, and refinement (also known as sophisticated). Whether it is business or socially, we all find ourselves in situations where we are meeting and greeting new people. The way you look, you speak, the way you carry yourself, your ability to be interested and interesting can spell the difference between being well received and not.

Etiquette is a set of rules we memorize. Manners express how much we care about other people their feelings and their needs. Etiquette rules are of the head, manners of the heart. Together they are a shield against embarrassment.

Social Graces to consider are:

1. Meeting and introducing - remember five "S" of meeting others – stand, smile, see (their eyes), shake and say (Hello John, I am happy to meet you).

2. On the telephone – always identify yourself immediately when making a telephone call. Try to answer with a smile.

3. Always learn to say "please" and "thank you" and experts say the encouragement to thank others and for things nicely is a must in our language and behaviors.

4. We must learn not to interrupt adults/friends when they are speaking

5. Using the phrase "excuse me" when they need attention, or when they bump into someone.

6. Keeping negative opinions to themselves (including funny facial expressions)

7. Knocking on closed doors before entering

8. Refraining from name-calling

9. Refraining from teasing

10. Covering their mouth when coughing and sneezing

11. Putting their napkins on their lap

12. Closing their mouth when chewing

13. Not raising their voice indoors

14. Greeting and saying goodbye when meeting or leaving someone.

15. Always write Thank you notes after receiving birthday gifts, and using correct internet manners

16. Being polite and forming relationships go hand in hand. People enjoy being in the company of those who are respectful.

17. We all like praise. Easy ways to show approval of through applause, verbal compliments, and sharing the accomplishments with others.

THE IMPACT OF SOCIAL GRACES IN BUSINESS

It is well known that others judge us by our actions. How they see us is important to success in life. There is a standard for the basic body of knowledge a well- educated person should have. Establishing a foundation of social grace, etiquette, manners, and politeness will go a long way towards success is in life both socially and in business. Good social grace never goes unnoticed.   People observe you carefully and minutely while you are in the public domain.

In business, one of the fundamental measures of success is the ability to build long-term, profitable relationships. These profits are not necessarily a reflection of just dollars and cents. Relationships can be profitable by measure of intangible assets,   such as knowledge, experience,   goodwill,   association and reputation.

Businesses and societies are created, built and sustained by people working together towards common goals. It is often equally important in driving towards these goals to rely on who you know, in addition to what you know.

In the quest for driving toward optimal outcomes in any relationship,   valuable connections begin by passing the initial test of making a good first impression. These early encounters are often evaluated by a person's conformity to cultural norms and social graces.

Social Graces that Impact Business Relationships

1. Listen Up / Goal: Be a Better Listener.

2. Make Eye Contact / Goal: Give Everyone Your Full Attention.

3. Be on Time / Goal: Be the First to Arrive.

4. Remember Names / Goal: Get the Name Right

5. Ignore Hearsay / Goal: Get the Facts.

6. Pass on Aggressive / Goal: Avoid Stubborn 'Know How'

7. Understand the Culture / Goal: Understand the Cultural Impact

8. Acknowledge and Respect / Goal: You Can Learn from Everyone

9. Thank You Matters Most / Goal: Always Give Thanks!

CHAPTER 2

THE ART OF LISTENING

The Art of Listening

Listening is the cornerstone of effective communication and, by extension, successful small talk. Effective listening means giving your full attention to the speaker, not just hearing their words. It involves being present in the moment, suspending judgment, and demonstrating empathy. When you listen actively, you pick up on verbal cues, emotions, and underlying messages, allowing you to respond thoughtfully and connect more deeply with others.

In social situations, one way to show you're offering your full attention is to listen in an engaged way. When you're in a conversation with someone, it should be equal parts talking and listening. When you're listening, show you're paying attention by practicing nonverbal cues like nodding and making eye contact with the speaker. It's also a good active listening practice to give small recaps of what someone just told you.

ACTIVE LISTENING: THE FOUNDATION OF MEANINGFUL CONVERSATION

Communication is at the heart of everything we do each day, whether at home, work or play. It involves talking and listening—actively – actively listening. Unfortunately, in today's technology-driven, fast-paced world, studies suggest many of us are spending less and less time to really listening to one another.

As an active listener, it's important to try to understand the message from the speaker's point of view. It includes letting the speaker know you're listening and you've understood what was said. Head nodding, smiles and eye contact are indications you're tuned in.

"We were given two ears but only one mouth, because listening is twice as hard as talking. "

- Epictetus (AD 55 – c. 135)

Mind you, this is not the same as hearing, which is a physical process where sound enters the eardrum and messages are passed to the brain. Rather, active listening can be described as an attitude that leads to listening for shared understanding. When we make a decision to actively listen, we listen for the content (the message) of what's being said as well as the attitude behind what's being said. Is the speaker happy, angry, excited, sad…or something else entirely?

Active listening encompasses the best of communication: actually hearing and understanding what's being said, processing the information and responding in order to clarify and elicit more information.

Active listening is the foundation of effective communication. It solves problems and resolves conflicts. It builds relationships and careers.

Develop and practice these six tips to boost your listening skills:

1. Make a Decision to Listen. Close your mind to clutter and noise, put away your smart phone and look at the person speaking to you. Give them your undivided attention.

2. Don't Interrupt. Make it a habit to let them finish what they're saying. Respect they have thoughts they're processing and speaking about, and wait to ask questions or make comments until they've finished.

3. Use Positive Body Language. The occasional nod, smile or hand/arm gesture shows you're listening to their every word. Avoid folding your arms across your chest as this may reflect defensiveness or disinterest.

4. Maintain Eye Contact. Keep your eyesfocused on the speaker and your earstuned to their voice. Don't get distracted and let your eyes wander.

5. Put Yourself in the Speaker's Shoes. Empathy is the heart and soul of good listening. If the person with whom you're talking to expresses sadness, anxiety or happiness, you, too, should convey the same feelings in your body language and words. This not only conveys you're a good listener but also shows respect.

6. Ask Questions throughout the Conversation. Asking questions show you're engaged and interested in what they have to say. Your ability to summarize and paraphrase will also demonstrate you hear them loud and clear.

STRATEGIES TO ENHANCE YOUR LISTENING SKILLS

Listening is an important skill to have in any professional setting and can be the difference between success and failure. Whether you're actively participating in meetings or simply observing the conversations, having strong listening skills will give you the edge.

In this blog post, we will discuss the best ways for developing listening skills in the workplace and provide some useful tips on how to put them into practice. We'll start by looking at why it's important to be a good listener and explore some of the strategies and techniques needed to become one.

Importance of listening in workplace communication

Communication in the workplace is an essential part of any successful business, and one skill that greatly enhances communication is effective listening. Listening can help build trust between colleagues, ensure clarity on projects and tasks, create a collaborative environment, and provide context for meaningful conversations.

As such, it's important for all working professionals to understand the importance of listening in workplace communication. In this section, we will discuss why listening is so critical to professional success.

1. Listening is essential for effective communication in the workplace

Listening is a key component of effective communication in the workplace. It is important to cultivate an environment where everyone feels heard and understood, as this encourages collaboration and sets a strong foundation for successful work performance.

Good listening skills in workplace communication also involve paying attention to nonverbal cues such as body language, facial expressions, and posture, which are all essential elements of effective communication. A healthy exchange of ideas begins by being attentive to others, actively engaging with their ideas, and taking in their perspective.

Being an engaged listener shows respect for others' expertise and can help create positive relationships among team members. Such practices are invaluable tools that help shape our workplace into an inspiring place to be.

2. Listening allows you to understand the other person's perspective and needs

Listening is an essential skill when engaging with others and can make a positive impact on relationships. Not only does it help build understanding, but it is also key to developing respect among peers. When we listen to someone else's perspective, we are able to foster a deeper understanding of their needs and intentions.

Conversely, taking time to consider our own thoughts and share them in meaningful ways builds trust and respect with others. Ultimately, listening allows us to create space for the meaningful dialogue which empowers relationships and opens up opportunities for collaboration on shared interests.

3. Listening builds trust and respect between coworkers

Actively listening to your coworkers builds strong relationships, fosters a spirit of collaboration, and enhances trust and respect between colleagues. It is essential to make sure that everyone involved in a discussion feels heard, validated, and respected for their contributions so that ideas can be exchanged in an open and honest way.

By really listening to our coworkers with an intent to understand, we create an environment of collaboration that encourages creative problem-solving and increases productivity. Listening doesn't only allow us to respond; it helps us develop meaningful relationships within the work environment.

4. Listening can help to prevent misunderstandings and conflict

When effective listening is practiced, confusing and unhelpful misunderstandings can be avoided, leading to fewer conflicts. Listening actively means not only taking in the words that are being said but also considering the underlying feelings of the speaker. Through careful observation of both body language and emotion, a listener can sometimes get an even better understanding of what their conversation partner is attempting to communicate.

It is important to remain sympathetic and open-minded when engaging in active listening; taking time to consider why someone may feel or think in a particular way can help build bridges between parties who may otherwise be at odds. As such, successful listening is often key to avoiding conflict and making sure all parties are on the same page.

5. Listening makes it more likely that the other person will listen to you in return

Listening is a skill that should be practiced in every facet of life, from discussions with colleagues to conversations with our friends and family. Listening shows respect and encourages communication, two essential elements of any successful exchange between two people. When we listen actively - rather than simply waiting for our turn to speak - it establishes openness and trust, which then sets the stage for the other person to willingly hear us when we have something to say.

By creating this foundation of mutual listening, energy is saved on both ends as the need to repeat oneself decreases along with any sense of frustration associated with being unheard. Ultimately, practicing good listening skills in workplace communication ensures that dialogue runs smoothly and efficiently.

6. Listening can help you to better understand your own thoughts and feelings

Listening is an often underrated strategy for understanding not only the thoughts and feelings of others but also our own. It has been said that true listening requires us to suspend judgment and be compassionate, empathetic, and open to learning new things.

By taking this approach when we listen – both to ourselves and others – we are able to uncover crucial information about our innermost thoughts and feelings, which can provide a deeper level of insight into our values, strengths, and shortcomings. Consequently, active listening can be invaluable in the pursuit of personal growth and greater self-understanding.

Best Ways for developing Good Businesses listening skills

Listening skills are an integral part of any successful workplace. Effective listening improves communication, enhances relationships, and increases the overall efficiency of the workplace. Developing listening skills is essential for any professional in order to be successful in their career.

1. Make a concerted effort to listen more than you speak

Listening to others is often a sorely overlooked talent in both professional and everyday settings. When we make an effort to listen more than we speak, we open ourselves up to new opportunities for learning and growth.

By allowing the speaker some space to be heard, we are paying attention to details that can help inform our conversations, decisions, and actions effectively.

Not only does this deepen our grasp of a situation or topic at hand, but it also fosters mutual respect and appreciation for one another's ideas. Taking the time to truly listen is not only beneficial for us but also creates a more productive environment where everyone involved feels included, valued, and respected.

2. Pay attention to both the words that are spoken and the body language of the speaker

Active listening goes beyond simply hearing words; it requires paying attention to both the actual words that are spoken, as well as the body language used by the speaker. While this is a different kind of skill set to possess than merely hearing with your ears, it's an important distinction that can help sharpen communication and understanding between two individuals.

Paying attention to both verbal and nonverbal cues increases attentiveness and accuracy in discerning what is really being said. The better you are able to pick up on these nuances in conversations, the more successful professional conversations will become for everyone involved.

3. Try to understand the speaker's point of view, even if you don't agree with it

Listening skills in workplace communication are the cornerstone of productive communication. Although you may find yourself in disagreement with someone's point of view, understanding it is essential to advancing conversations and preserving relationships. Listening with an open mind and actively trying to comprehend where the speaker is coming from can not only provide insight into their perspectives but also build trust between both parties. Listening is a skill that requires patience, effort, and practice—but it's one worth mastering in order to improve communication.

4. Ask questions to clarify points that you don't understand

As part of our professional development and communication in the workplace, it is important to foster an environment that encourages dialogue. Listening skills are essential if we want to proactively share our thoughts and ideas. When questions arise, it is only natural to clarify any points that we don't fully understand.

Asking questions allows us to engage in meaningful conversations and have a deeper level of understanding of each other's perspectives. Additionally, it allows us to collaborate more effectively and facilitates better decision-making. Let's commit to using our voice by asking questions when needed; this will be inclusive of all members of the team.

5. Repeat back what you have heard to ensure that you have accurately understood the message.

Listening skills are critical when striving to accurately understand and remember what has been said. One simple yet effective way of doing this is to periodically repeat back the message you have heard.

Doing this demonstrates active listening and ensures both parties that the information has been properly absorbed, avoiding any unnecessary confusion or misunderstanding. Ultimately, the end goal of clear communication is achieved through such a strategy by providing understanding and mutual agreement between all involved.

6. **Avoid interrupting the speaker, even if you think you know what they are going to say.**

Listening without interrupting is beneficial to both the speaker and listener, allowing the speaker to express their thoughts fully, and allowing the listener to gain an understanding of the other person's point of view. Listening attentively shows respect, demonstrates your understanding and appreciation of the speaker's ideas, and can help build stronger relationships in both work and personal settings.

Listening prevents misunderstandings by allowing you as the listener to accurately evaluate what is being said. When you think you know what a speaker is going to say or agree with a point before they finish speaking, resist any urge you might have to interrupt them; be patient and remain open-minded; allow them to finish so that you maintain a good rapport and prevent potential conflict.

7. Avoid distractions, such as your phone or other electronic devices.

Listening carefully is a critical skill in the workplace and life overall, as it enables us to properly understand and absorb information that comes our way. To maximise our listening skills in workplace communication, it's important to avoid distractions, such as relying on electronic devices like phones and tablets. Not only do these devices provide a constant flow of messages and notifications, but they can also be incredibly distracting when utilised during meetings or conversations. Make sure to consciously put away your phone during meetings or conversations to ensure you're in tune with what's going on and optimise your potential for success.

8. Make eye contact with the speaker and maintain an open-body posture.

Listening skills are an important part of any successful communication, and making eye contact with the speaker and having an open body posture are two great ways to demonstrate that you are actively engaged in the conversation.

Making eye contact with the speaker helps ensure that you pay attention to their words and helps them feel heard while having an open-body posture communicates that you are relaxed and comfortable in the conversation.

Showing these behaviors lets the other person know that their insights and opinions matter, making it easier for both parties to have a productive interaction.

9. Be patient and refrain from finishing the speaker's sentences for them.

Listening can often require a great deal of patience, particularly when a speaker may not finish their thought or be speaking more slowly than we are used to. It requires us to understand that speakers take time to find the right words and could benefit from your patience rather than you jumping in to complete their sentences.

Refraining from finishing other people's sentences demonstrates respect and helps show that we are committed and engaged with what they have said. Listening fully and attentively will only lead to more productive conversations, making it essential that when engaging with someone else, we all remember the importance of taking the time to listen attentively before responding.

10. Allow silences in the conversation, as they can often be helpful in processing information.

It is important to practice good listening skills in workplace communication in any sort of conversation, and allowing silence can be an effective tool in doing so. We often don't realise that we need time to understand the conversation, but this isn't mistaken for a lack of interest or compassion – instead, it is considered a sign of respect towards the person who's speaking.

Granted, some silences are awkward, but most people appreciate being heard and feel more comfortable when they have time to pause and process what has been said. Listening has been proven to improve relationships, reduce conflicts, encourage better communication and ensure that all parties walk away feeling heard and respected. Allow silences in the conversation where appropriate - they may just be your savior!

Wrapping It Up

Good listening skills in business communication are essential to success in the workplace. Active listening allows individuals to better understand their teammates, colleagues, and customers. It helps to foster strong relationships and build trust. By practicing active listening, one can become a better listener and be able to more effectively receive and process information from others.

This will help them to make better decisions, increase productivity, and even reduce misunderstandings and conflicts. Therefore, it is important for everyone to develop their listening skills and practice active listening techniques in the workplace.

CHAPTER 3

INITIATING CONVERSATIONS WITH CONFIDENCE

The hardest part of socializing, for many people, is how to start a conversation.

However, it is a big mistake to go about life not making the first move and waiting for someone else to do it (in conversation or anything).

This isn't to say you must always be the first in everything or initiate a conversation with everyone you see. What should be said, though, is once you get good at starting conversations, a lot of other things will progress in the way you want; such as networking and your love life.

According to a research study by the National Library of Medicine, social interaction is a great contributor to good health and longevity. [1]

Starting a conversation doesn't have to be purely physical. Thanks to rapid technological advancement and the pandemic, people have embraced online communication. Here are a few simple tips on how to start a conversation.

Benefits of Learning How to Start a Conversation

The first thing is you should acknowledge why it is a good thing to be able to initiate conversations with strangers or people who you don't know well:

You look more approachable if you are comfortable approaching others.

Meeting new people physically or on social media means developing a network of friends or peers which leads to more knowledge and experiences.

You explore beyond the perimeters of your comfort zone

You can only learn so much alone, and I'm sure you're aware of the benefits of learning from others. Being able to distinguish the 'good from bad' amongst a group of people will help in building a suitable network, or making a fun night.

All people are good in their own way. Being able to have a good time with anybody is a worthy trait and something to discuss another time. However, if you have a specific purpose while in social situations, you may want to stick with people who are suitable.

This means distinguishing between people who might suit you and your 'purpose' from those who probably won't. This can require some people-judging, which I am generally very opposed to. However, this does make approaching people all the more easier.

It helps to motivate the conversation if you really want to know this person. Also, you'll find your circle of friends and peers grows to something you really like and enjoy.

Building Confidence

The most important part of starting a conversation with someone you don't know physically or virtually is, arguably, having confidence. It should be obvious that without any amount of self-esteem you will struggle.

Having confidence in yourself and who you are makes this job very easy.

If you find yourself doubting your worth, or how interesting you are, make a few mental notes of why you are interesting and worth talking to. There is no question you are. You just have to realize that.

What do I do? What is interesting about it? What are my strong points and what are my weak ones? Confident people succeed because they've learned the art of starting a conversation with strangers and using their strengths.

APPROACHING STRANGERS: STARTING A CONVERSATION WITH EASE

Human beings are social creatures. What this means is that for any relationship to be productive or successful, there needs to be a level of social interaction and communication. It is only through communication that we can make our thoughts known and form meaningful relationships with the people around us. Hence, the need for effective social skills in modern society.

Oftentimes, what determines the way a person is viewed or the opportunities they are exposed to is their ability to express themselves and utilize social skills to make their thoughts known. Not everyone has the ability to form relationships with strangers. This is why so many talented people are not taken as seriously as they should be.

In many leadership roles, people look out for individuals who are charismatic, bold and charming, people who are quick on their feet and can strike up a conversation with a stranger they have never met before.

Due to several factors, some people are unable to engage in the most mundane conversations with people they don't know. This can lead others to write them off as inept or inefficient, but it is important to understand that personalities differ and some have a harder time than others when it comes to interpersonal relationship skills.

If you fall into the category of people who are unsure how to talk to strangers or people you have never met, there is nothing to be ashamed of. Millions of people are uncomfortable with strangers as well.

One of the advantages of living in a digital world is that you have renewed access to resources and technology that can help you gain any skills you require in your own time. One of such resources you can utilize to improve your social skills is digital coaching.

The Science of Conversation

Communication forms the backbone of any human interaction. The efficacy of a relationship is dependent on how well all parties can make their thoughts known and pass their message across to a listener or an observer.

Without realizing it, our brains process all kinds of information from the people we interact with on a daily basis. Our interactions form patterns that are interpreted by the subconscious mind, creating a base for any future interactions. This is why it is important to be conscious of the way we communicate with the people we try to form relationships with.

There are different kinds of communication that influence the way we interact with people. Communication can be either verbal or nonverbal and both are equally important in creating relationships.

Most people do not realize that nonverbal communication is an efficient means of passing messages across without saying anything. People you talk to notice your body language, the way you act and the things you do, even when they are actively listening. Behaviors can often reveal more truth than words, even when you don't intend them to. Relationships are made stronger when actions match words no matter the situation.

Even when engaging in conversation as a means of communication, it is important to practice empathy and actively listen to people. Human beings are more likely to open up and trust when they know that they will be listened to.

As much as we may want to ensure that people hear us out, we also need to be careful to ensure that we don't make others feel insignificant. Demonstrate empathy and really listen to people. You'd be shocked at how easily they open up when they know that you are interested in their thoughts, needs and desires.

Overcoming the Fear of Rejection

The fear of rejection is a major factor that prevents people from making connections with others. In a public place, the fear of rejection may stop you from approaching a stranger, even if you find them attractive. Several people suffer from the fear of rejection, whether they realize it or not, and more often than not, it could lead to regrets.

There are many reasons why an individual could have a fear of rejection, and it can get worse if left unattended for a long time.

Admittedly, it is not easy to eliminate the fear of rejection at once, but there are tips that could help make it easier.

Enhanced self-regulation: Self-regulation refers to a person's ability to recognize and bring their emotional responses under conscious control. The more able you are to identify negative thoughts and feelings such as fear, the more likely you are to find solutions that work.

Build resilience: This is the ability and willingness to keep moving forward in spite of challenges that make the situation difficult. Resilience will make it possible for you to talk to a complete stranger in spite of the fear you feel.

Facing your fears: Some of us are prone to using avoidance as a way of dealing with problems, including the fear of rejection. However, this does more harm than good in the long run. You only push your problems down instead of finding a solution.

Techniques for Starting a Conversation with Strangers

There is no specific rule book to follow when starting conversations with strangers. Each person is different and we all respond to interactions in unique ways. Still, some conversation starters can be used to break the ice and make people more comfortable when meeting for the first time.

1. Offer compliments: Everyone loves a compliment. People want to know that they are doing something right and sincere compliments can help cross the hurdle of finding a good enough conversation starter.

2. Introduce yourself: Some people are more likely to engage in a conversation with you when they know who you are. Not everyone is comfortable starting a conversation with someone they don't know. Introducing yourself makes it easier for the other party to introduce themselves as well and begin a conversation.

3. Ask for input: Asking a stranger for advice is a great way to set a subject matter that you can both discuss. Asking for their input makes them feel important. It also displays your humility and readiness to learn.

4. Jokes: Laughter helps to build bonds among people. A light, polite joke and a bit of a laugh tends to gently lay down a

person's defenses, making them more open and responsive to the conversation.

Asking a lot of questions can help you find a common ground with a stranger, making it easier to prolong the interaction and make a memorable impression.

Digital coaching can help you practice and get used to modern communication techniques or improve your social skills. Everyone needs a bit of help in adopting efficient communication strategies that make interactions easier. Digital coaching can provide that assistance and help you improve the quality of your relationships.

Building Rapport and Making Connections

Genuine connections are made with people when there is mutual regard from each party. It would be hard to create a rapport with someone you have no regard for. Forming a rapport takes effort and patience. You can't create a meaningful relationship out of thin air. There needs to be a common ground where both parties feel comfortable enough to express themselves and exchange ideas. By listening and being empathetic in your responses, you stand a higher chance of leaving a memorable impression.

Showing people that you pay attention helps to build trust, which is one of the pillars of a good relationship. It also makes it easier to discover things you have in common with the stranger.

Granted, a lot of these things seem easier said than done, but they are techniques that can be learned and acquired through digital coaching. You can build your social skills and become adept at conversations by utilizing an efficient digital coaching program that focuses on your communication difficulties and guides you on how to overcome them.

ELEVATING YOUR INTRODUCTION: CRAFTING AN IMPRESSIVE SELF-INTRODUCTION

How to introduce yourself professionally

Here are four ways you can introduce yourself professionally:

1. State your purpose

Many people introduce themselves by stating their name and current job title, but you should also try to add information your new contact can't find on your business card. If you are at a networking event, consider starting with your name, then stating what your passion is. You could also mention what your goal is for the encounter, such as finding someone to collaborate with on a new idea you have.

Quickly summarize who you are and why you are there when you interview for a job. Your interviewers already know what position you are applying for, so have your professional introduction explain your purpose in a few sentences. You should include your name and why you are a good candidate for the job position.

Keep in mind that you should start your introduction in a way that is appropriate for the context. For example, if you're at a networking event you might simply start by shaking a new connection's hand and giving them your first and last name. Then begin a conversation by asking and answering questions about their background and your own.

2. Consider your body language

When you introduce yourself to someone, you can demonstrate confidence by speaking in a clear and audible voice and communicating a positive attitude through nonverbal cues. During your conversation, maintain natural body language to show you are open.

3. Explain why you are valuable

Employers might schedule multiple interviews throughout the day or week for a job opening. Your professional introduction should convey your unique experience and qualifications so you stand out from other candidates. Hearing an introduction that sounds different from previous ones directs your new contact's attention toward you and tends to make it more memorable. During an interview introduction, for example, you should let your interviewer know why you would make a valuable contribution to the team.

4. Understand the culture

Consider researching the company before an interview or meeting to understand their culture. Before an introduction with a computer programming company, for example, review their website or social media pages to see what the culture is like. If the company seems more casual, it may be appropriate to include humor in your introduction. For a more formal position or meeting with a potential client, keeping a more professional demeanor could make you more likely to be hired or gain the client's business.

Structuring your introduction

In professional settings, a good introduction doesn't need to be formulaic and can be casual or lengthy, depending on the scenario. Here's a general outline for an intro that covers all the bases:

- **BEGINNING**

If you're wondering how to start an introduction about yourself, the best thing to do is keep it simple. Greet your conversation partner or audience, state your name, and mention why you're there, if relevant.

- Background

Let your audience know where you're from and what you've been up to recently. Customize this to the situation. In some cases, you'll discuss where you grew up and where you live now. In others, where you went to school and your profession will be your focus.

- Skills

In professional settings, mention any relevant skills and offer context by discussing why you're mentioning or where you gained them.

If this is a written introduction, like a cover letter or letter of intent, include skills mentioned in the job description to show you've prepared and know what's required for the role. And ensuring your skills are aligned benefits you. According to Gallup, working where you can use your skills to the best of your ability reduces the likelihood of hypertension and high cholesterol.

- Achievements

In most professional intros, it's helpful to note things you've accomplished, like degrees or promotions. This might also be relevant when introducing yourself to new colleagues or clients.

- Ambitions

You can use an introduction to express to your community what you'd like to achieve and how you might get there. This subtle type of networking might help you gain help or land an opportunity you might've missed.

To show your proactivity and sincerity, include examples of how you're already taking action to realize these goals. For example, if you're interested in learning French, mention you're taking classes and have a language-exchange partner you meet once a week.

- Values

Expressing your values during an introduction doesn't have to be explicit. The way you behave when meeting someone says more than stating you value a specific trait. Be honest, speak articulately and with kindness, and remain humble to show you value transparency, compassion, and humility.

If this is a job search or workplace introduction, align your values with those expressed by the team or company. For example, if their mission statement mentions valuing teamwork skills, talk about your love of collaborating with others to achieve common goals.

How to create a great self-introduction

Preparing a succinct and genuine introduction is valuable in every facet of your life. Here are five tips for composing the best introduction:

1. REHEARSE IT

A great way to make introducing yourself less nerve-wracking is to memorize a simple introduction. Customize this to each situation so you don't have to think on the spot so much, or rehearse intros for various scenarios so you're never caught off guard.

Try recording yourself saying the introduction to ensure you're speaking articulately and clearly. You could also rehearse it with a friend to get constructive feedback.

2. TELL A STORY

Instead of summarizing easily-accessible online information about you, engage your audience by sprinkling in new details and formatting your intro like a story.

A great way to do this is to replicate the STAR interview method. This is the framework:

Situation: Establish your career path, starting with where you came from and a challenge you faced.

Task: Define what your position and responsibilities were during this time.

Action: Tell them how you confronted this challenge.

Result: Share what you achieved and the insights you gained along the way.

You can shorten or lengthen this story, depending on your circumstances.

3. COMMUNICATE YOUR VALUES

Communication skills are essential to making a good first impression. Demonstrate your confidence with good posture, show your values by remaining sincere, and express your consideration for others by actively listening.

4. SHOWCASE YOUR PERSONALITY

Even in professional settings, your audience wants to know what kind of person you are. A hiring manager cares about your qualifications but also wants to ensure you'll get along with your coworkers and enjoy the company culture.

Being yourself also shows your sincerity — you're not about to completely hide qualities such as humor and nerdiness just because this is a formal introduction.

5.   END WITH A QUESTION

A great way to show your interest in the person on the other end is to complete your introduction with a question. In a professional setting, this might be asking something about a job description or probing about next steps. This shows you see them as active participants in the conversation and also keeps things moving smoothly.

CHAPTER 4

NAVIGATING CAUSAL CONVERSATION

Navigating causal conversation is a valuable skill that can greatly enhance your social interactions, whether in personal or professional settings. Causal conversation serves as a bridge to deeper connections and can pave the way for more meaningful conversations.

Navigating causal conversation is an art that involves careful observation, active listening, and a genuine interest in others. By mastering the subtleties of this essential skill, you can create more comfortable and meaningful interactions, whether in your personal relationships or professional endeavors. Causal conversation is not just about words; it's about building bridges and fostering connections that can lead to lasting and significant relationships.

In this extensive exploration, we'll delve into the art of navigating causal conversation, providing insights and strategies for mastering this essential aspect of communication.

1. Understanding the Purpose of Causal conversation:

Causal conversation serves several vital functions. It establishes rapport, breaks the ice, and helps people feel more comfortable in each other's presence. It can also gather information about a person's interests, background, and current mood. Understanding these purposes is crucial for navigating causal conversation effectively.

2. Choosing Appropriate Topics:

The key to successful causal conversation lies in selecting appropriate topics that resonate with your conversation partner. Begin with neutral subjects like the weather, current events, or common experiences. As the conversation progresses, gradually explore more personal or specific topics based on the other person's cues.

3. Active Listening:

As discussed earlier, Active listening is a cornerstone of navigating causal conversation. It involves not only hearing but also understanding and responding thoughtfully to what the other person is saying. Show genuine interest by maintaining eye contact, nodding, and asking follow-up questions based on their comments.

4. Body Language:

Your body language plays a significant role in navigating causal conversation. Maintain open and approachable body language, such as smiling, maintaining good posture, and using gestures sparingly. Avoid crossing your arms or appearing disinterested, as this can hinder the flow of conversation.

5. Asking Open-Ended Questions:

One of the most effective techniques in causal conversation is asking open-ended questions. These questions invite the other person to share more about themselves, fostering a deeper connection. Instead of asking, "Did you have a good weekend?" try "What did you do over the weekend?" This encourages a more detailed response.

6. **Listening for Cues and Shared Interests**:

As the conversation unfolds, pay close attention to cues and shared interests. Look for common ground or experiences that you can explore further. Shared interests provide natural conversational pathways and create a sense of connection.

7. Providing Validation and Empathy:

People appreciate validation and empathy in small talk. Acknowledge their feelings or experiences with statements like, "I can understand how that might be challenging, " or "That sounds like a fantastic experience. " This shows that you value their perspective and feelings.

8. Avoiding Controversial Topics:

While causal conversation can delve into personal experiences, it's essential to avoid controversial or sensitive topics, such as politics or religion, unless you are certain they are safe subjects for discussion. These topics can quickly lead to disagreements and disrupt the flow of the conversation.

9. Transitioning to Deeper Conversations:

Navigating causal conversation skillfully can pave the way for more meaningful discussions. When you sense that the other person is comfortable and engaged, you can gradually transition to deeper topics by asking questions that invite reflection or sharing personal anecdotes.

10. Exiting Gracefully:

Knowing when and how to exit a causal conversation is equally important. If the conversation has reached a natural conclusion, express appreciation for the chat, offer a warm farewell, and potentially suggest reconnecting in the future. Avoid abrupt endings or lingering in uncomfortable silences.

11. Practice and Patience:

Navigating causal conversation is a skill that improves with practice. Don't be discouraged by occasional awkward moments or unsuccessful attempts. Embrace each interaction as an opportunity to refine your causal conversation skills and build better connections.

CAUSAL CONVERSATION AS A BRIDGE TO DEEPER CONNECTIONS

Causal conversation, often dismissed as trivial or superficial, is in fact a powerful bridge to deeper connections in both personal and professional relationships. It serves as the initial stepping stone, allowing individuals to gradually build trust, rapport, and intimacy.

Causal conversationis a potent tool for building bridges to deeper connections. It provides the initial context for getting to know someone and gradually transitioning into more profound discussions. By employing active listening, empathy, and thoughtful questions, you can harness the power of causal conversation to create lasting and meaningful relationships in both your personal and professional life.

Moving on to the significance of causal conversation as a bridge to deeper connections and uncover strategies for using it effectively.

The Role of Causal conversation:

1. Building Trust:

Trust is the cornerstone of any meaningful relationship. Causal conversation provides a safe and non-threatening environment for individuals to get to know each other gradually. Through casual conversations about neutral topics, trust begins to develop.

2. Breaking the Ice:

In unfamiliar settings or when meeting new people, causal conversation acts as an essential icebreaker. It eases tension and discomfort, making it easier for individuals to open up and engage in more profound conversations.

3. Discovering Common Ground:

Causal conversation allows individuals to discover shared interests, experiences, or perspectives. Finding common ground creates a sense of connection and provides conversational fodder for deeper discussions.

Transitioning from Causal Conversation to Deeper Conversations:

1. Listen for Clues:

During causal conversation, listen for cues or hints that the other person is comfortable and interested in delving deeper. They may reveal personal stories or express curiosity about your experiences.

2. Ask Permission:

When transitioning to a more profound topic, it's considerate to ask if the other person is comfortable discussing it. For instance, you can say, "I've really enjoyed our conversation so far. Would you mind if we talked about something a bit more personal?"

3. Share Vulnerability:

To foster deeper connections, consider sharing some vulnerability or personal anecdotes. This can encourage the other person to reciprocate, creating a deeper bond based on trust and authenticity.

4. Ask Thoughtful Questions:

Pose thoughtful and reflective questions that invite deeper contemplation. Questions like "What's your greatest passion in life?" or "What has been your most significant life lesson?" encourage meaningful sharing.

Causal Conversation Professional Settings:

Causal conversation is equally relevant in professional settings. It can serve as the foundation for strong working relationships, partnerships, and collaborations. Effective causal conversation can help you establish trust with colleagues, superiors, or clients, ultimately leading to more productive and harmonious professional connections.

MASTERING THE ART OF CAUSAL CONVERSATION

How do you feel about causal conversation? Have you ever been to a networking event and spent the best part of the evening hovering by the buffet table because you felt unsure of how to strike up a conversation? Perhaps the thought of having to endure another dinner party struggling to find something new to say makes you break out in a cold sweat?

Maybe you fall into the camp that views small talk as a necessary evil that has to be endured before you can move the conversation onto a deeper level? Talking about the weather or the latest Netflix drama may seem like a waste of time but these small interactions can be the building blocks for deeper connections. Learning to embrace, and even enjoy, causal conversation, which can also be called small talks, can do wonders for your personal and professional life. Whether you are at a networking event, dinner party or on a first date, mastering the art of small talk will open up new opportunities and help you form authentic relationships.

If you struggle with causal conversation because you are socially anxious or find it hard to think of things to say, here are some tips to help you grow in confidence.

1. Adopt a growth mindset

Don't worry if causal conversation doesn't come naturally to you. With the right mindset, anyone can learn to be a good conversationalist. In particular, a growth mindset will help you step out of your comfort zone and stay motivated when you face challenges. People with a growth mindset believe that they can improve with practice whereas those with a fixed mindset think that a person's traits and abilities are determined at birth.

2. Find opportunities to practice

Don't sit around waiting for new people to come and talk to you. Instead, create opportunities to make causal conversation by actively approaching strangers. Once you accept that you find small talk challenging, you can take responsibility for improving your skills and actively seek out opportunities to change your behaviour.

3. Be an active participant

Having a conversation can be likened to two people hitting a tennis ball back and forth. The serve is when you initiate the conversation and a good rally involves both parties contributing equally to the exchange.

The objective is not to outplay your conversational partner but rather to keep the ball going backwards and forwards. If you want to be a better conversationalist, you have to be a willing and active participant and not leave the work of maintaining the conversation to the other person.

4. Use body language to establish rapport

Use your body language throughout the conversation to show that you are interested and engaged. Visual cues are especially important when you are listening to the other person. Make eye contact, smile (unless the topic being discussed is of a serious or sombre nature) and stay focused on the speaker.

Try not to cross your arms or put your hands on your hips and avoid fidgeting or looking across the room to see what other people are doing. Show that you are listening by nodding, humming and asking elaborating questions.

5. Prepare some ice-breakers

Preparation is a key part of making causal conversation both easier and more enjoyable. It is natural to be nervous when starting a conversation and many people feel more comfortable if they have some go-to icebreakers up their sleeve. Here are a few suggestions:

Use the situation, venue or event as your starting point. For example: "What brings you here today?" or "What did you think of the concert/play/lecture?"

Pay the other person a compliment. For example: "I love your shoes. It is great to see someone wearing colour. "

Find some common ground. For example: "I work in marketing too. How long have you been in the industry?"

6. Be an active listener

You might think that you are a good listener but in a conversation are you really concentrating on what the other person is saying or are you just waiting for an opportunity to speak? If someone is describing their recent holiday, it can be tempting to jump in with a vacation-related anecdote of your own as soon as they stop to take a breath.

Being an active listener means listening to understand rather than to respond. The next time you talk to someone, resist the impulse to turn the focus onto yourself. Instead, reflect on what is being said and ask relevant questions that invite the other person to expand on the topic.

7. Ask open-ended questions

Try to ask open-ended questions rather than close-ended questions that only require a 'yes' or 'no' answer. For instance instead of asking 'do you like your job?' you could say ' How did you get into your field of work?' or 'what do you like most about your job? ' People generally like talking about themselves but beware of asking questions that are too personal when you are still at the getting to know each other stage.

8. Steer clear of heavy topics

The point of small talk is to keep it light. Avoid sensitive and potentially controversial topics such as politics, religion or money. As well as discussing your surroundings, other good small talk topics include entertainment (TV shows, movies, books, plays etc.), art and culture, sports and travel. Here in the UK, the weather is a very popular small talk topic and while it may not seem like the most exciting conversation starter, it is definitely a safe subject when talking to new people.

9. Finish on a note of gratitude

If you're new to small talk, ending a conversation can seem as tricky as starting it. Debra Fine suggests that when it is time to leave, you should thank the other person for their time, expertise or simply say how much you enjoyed talking to them.

Expressing gratitude will not only leave the other person feeling good about themselves, but also boosts the likelihood of building a long-term connection. If you would like to see the person again, you should say so and follow up with an email, text or phone call within the next day or two.

CHAPTER 5

BEYOND CAUSAL CONVERSATIONS: BUILDING GENUINE CONNECTIONS

In an increasingly connected world today, building and nurturing relationships are more important than ever. And while it's tempting to focus on the big picture, which seems to be the business strategy, the marketing campaign, or the sales pitch, it is equally important not to overlook the little things, like small talk.

People often think small talk is silly or pointless, but it's a powerful way to build trust. Whether you meet someone for the first time or catch up with an old friend, small talk can help you find common ground and ultimately create meaningful relationships.

So why is small talk so important? For starters, it helps break the ice. When you meet someone for the first time, small talk can help ease the tension and create a more relaxed, friendly atmosphere. It also gives you a chance to get to know the other person on a more personal level—to find out what they're interested in, what their hobbies are, and what they do for fun.

But small talk isn't just about making a good first impression. It's also a way to build rapport and establish trust over time. By showing a genuine interest in the other person and sharing a little bit about yourself, you can create a sense of familiarity and connection that can be invaluable in business and in life.

Of course, not all small talk is created equal. Some people are naturally gifted at making small talk, while others struggle to find the right words. If you're in the latter category, don't worry; small talk is a skill that can be learned and developed over time.

THE POWER OF AUTHENTICITY

At the heart of every successful business lies a set of core values. These guiding principles help drive decision-making, shape company culture, and form the foundation upon which the company operates. And in today's fast-paced business world, the value of authenticity has never been more important.

Authenticity is more than just a buzzword – it's a way of life. It involves being true to yourself, your values, and your intentions. Whether you're an entrepreneur, a business leader or a professional, embracing the power of authenticity can help you connect with people on a deeper level, build meaningful relationships, and take your business and personal growth to new heights.

Authenticity is a powerful force that can have a profound impact on your personal and professional life. By embracing authenticity and its core values of vulnerability and transparency, you can connect more deeply with others, build meaningful relationships, and achieve success in your endeavors.

Let's delve into the concepts of authenticity, vulnerability, and transparency, and explore how these values can influence success in business and personal growth.

The first step to embracing authenticity is understanding what it means. At its core, authenticity is about being real. It involves being genuine, honest, and transparent in all aspects of your life. This means letting go of any facades or illusions you might be holding onto and getting comfortable with who you truly are.

One of the keys to living an authentic life is embracing vulnerability. Vulnerability is often seen as a weakness, but in reality, it's a strength. When you allow yourself to be vulnerable, you open yourself up to new experiences, deeper connections, and greater opportunities for growth. When you're vulnerable, you invite others to do the same, creating a culture of trust, openness, and authenticity

Transparency is also essential to authenticity. Transparency means being open and honest about what you're doing, how you're doing it, and why you're doing it. It's about being clear and forthright in your communications, both in your personal and professional life. By being transparent, you build trust, credibility, and respect, which are essential to success in business and personal growth.

One of the biggest benefits of authenticity is that it allows you to connect with people on a deeper level. When you're authentic, people feel like they can trust you. They feel like they know the real you, which creates a sense of intimacy and connection that's hard to replicate otherwise.

This sense of connection can be incredibly powerful in business. It allows you to build long-lasting relationships with clients, customers, and colleagues, which can help fuel your growth and success over the long term. In addition, authenticity can help you stand out in a crowded marketplace. When you're real, people are more likely to remember you, recommend you, and work with you again in the future.

Authenticity Builds Loyalty

People don't want to learn just about your business; they want to know who you are and who they are buying from. Humans desire emotional connection.

This way, when they choose you as their go-to provider for whatever product or service you offer, they know their money is going towards something or someone that has to mean for them. That's how you build loyalty.

Sure, the experience and quality of your services matter, but that feeling or proximity makes the difference. They believe in your brand.

How You Cultivate Authenticity

Your content reflects how you and your brand are, so it should always be genuine, honest, and human-centered to make meaningful connections with customers. By sharing what you care about, you become authentic.

- **Don't be something you are not:**

Don't try to be something that you are not. If you focus on becoming like other, more successful businesses, you will lose your essence.

- **Trust your instinct**

your brand will benefit from having a personality; people will recognize it and want to do business with you. However, if this personality constantly changes, they will go somewhere else.

Trust your instinct. This is the best way to stay true to your brand personality. Turn down opportunities that you don't feel right or don't fit your brand. Be faithful to your story.

- **Stand out from the rest:**

Use your uniqueness as an advantage; how you are and what you believe can become a personality trait for your brand, and people love that. They will remember things you say, phrases you often use, or silly expressions that accompany your brand.

All this will make you stand out from the rest of your competition.

DEEPENING RELATIONSHIPS THROUGH VULNERABILITY

Embracing vulnerability is a key to living an authentic life as earlier mentioned.

Vulnerability can be defined as the willingness and capacity to open oneself up emotionally, share personal experiences, thoughts, and feelings, and be authentic in interactions with others. It involves a degree of transparency and honesty that goes beyond surface-level communication, allowing for a deeper and more genuine connection to be established.

In this book, vulnerability plays a pivotal role in building trust, fostering empathy, and nurturing meaningful relationships. It encourages individuals to share their true selves, including their fears, aspirations, and challenges, in a way that invites reciprocity and mutual understanding. Embracing vulnerability empowers individuals to connect on a deeper level, both personally and professionally, ultimately leading to more profound and lasting connections that can benefit their business growth and personal development.

Vulnerability is a power tool in an emotionally intelligent leader's toolkit. Courageous leaders leverage their "woundedness" into genuine connections, innovation and learning. They embrace moments of vulnerability by acknowledging their current state, taking responsibility for their emotions and asking for help.

If vulnerabilities are left unchecked, energy is invested in ways to combat your perceived weaknesses. Your wounds get buried deeper.

Blame, defensiveness or shame block you from taking appropriate risks, creativity is squashed, and innovation is eradicated.

Hiding vulnerabilities is exhausting. It is like being a secret agent, and no one must know. Hiding or protecting your vulnerabilities is driven by a mistaken belief that you are not strong enough to handle the challenges.

Let me share with you some ways to open the door to vulnerability in business.

1. How can l help?

Genuine connections are formed when you are open about your experiences. I'm not talking about the blanket rule that discloses all your personal secrets. What I am referring to are the vulnerable moments when life gets in the way.

2. Take off the armor.

Vulnerability fuels the strongest relationships and can transform performance to help bring more success to an organization. Being vulnerable at work and in business simply means you are ready to take the armor off, put aside any pretenses, and check your ego at the door.

3. Creating a vulnerability mind shift.

Start to see the aspirations of the business through the eyes of your customers. As you step back and allow others to take the driver's seat of conversations, your customers will feel more connected, invested and a deep sense of commitment to the shared vision of the organization.

To build trust, business owners must work with a power of transparency, accountability and vulnerability.

4. When people share, great business is done.

Vulnerability is hardly a trait many running a business race to embrace, yet it can build deeper relationships, loyalty and enable people to bring their whole selves to work.

CHAPTER 6

THE IMPORTANCE OF SOCIAL GRACE TO CAUSAL CONVERSATION

As earlier discussed in this book, Social graces are skills used to interact politely in social situations. They include manners and etiquette, which are specifically accepted rules within a culture for the application of universal manners.

Social grace is the invisible thread that weaves through the fabric of small talk, transforming ordinary conversations into meaningful exchanges. Its importance lies in its ability to create an environment of respect, trust, and authenticity, ultimately enriching relationships and fostering personal and professional growth. When small talk is infused with social grace, it becomes a powerful tool for creating connections that can leave a positive and lasting impact on both individuals involved.

The importance of social grace in the context of causal conversation cannot be overstated. Social grace encompasses a set of skills and behaviors that allow individuals to navigate social interactions with poise, consideration, and respect. When applied to small talk, social grace plays a crucial role in elevating these seemingly casual conversations to a higher level of quality and effectiveness. Here's an exploration of why social grace is essential to causal conversations:

1. Creating a Positive Atmosphere:

Social grace sets the tone for a positive and welcoming atmosphere during causal conversation. It involves being polite, attentive, and considerate of the other person's feelings and perspectives. When both parties in a conversation exhibit social grace, it creates a comfortable and enjoyable environment that encourages open communication.

2. Building Trust and Rapport:

Trust is the foundation of any meaningful relationship, and causal conversation is no exception. Social grace helps individuals build trust by demonstrating respect, honesty, and authenticity. When people feel respected and valued in a conversation, they are more likely to open up and share meaningful insights.

3. Fostering Genuine Connections:

Causal conversation can be a bridge to deeper connections, and social grace facilitates this transition. By showing genuine interest in the other person, actively listening, and asking thoughtful questions, individuals can use small talk as a means to explore shared interests and experiences, paving the way for more profound and authentic connections.

4. Resolving Misunderstandings:

Misunderstandings and miscommunications can arise even in casual conversations. Social grace equips individuals with the skills to address these issues gracefully. It encourages clarifying questions, empathy, and a willingness to resolve any tensions or confusions that may arise during small talk.

5. Encouraging Reciprocity:

Causal conversation often involves a degree of reciprocity, where both parties take turns sharing and listening. Social grace encourages balanced participation, ensuring that each person feels heard and valued. This balanced exchange fosters a sense of equality in the conversation, reinforcing the connection.

6. Navigating Delicate Topics:

In causal conversation, individuals may unintentionally venture into sensitive or potentially contentious territory. Social grace helps individuals navigate these situations with sensitivity and tact, avoiding arguments or discomfort while keeping the conversation flowing harmoniously.

7. Leaving a Positive Impression:

A fundamental aspect of social grace is the ability to leave a positive impression on others. In causal conversation this skill is invaluable. People remember how they felt during a conversation,   and when social grace is employed,   it leaves a lasting impression of respect, kindness, and consideration.

8. Adapting to Diverse Audiences:

Effective causal conversation often requires adapting to diverse audiences, each with their unique backgrounds,   preferences,   and communication styles.   Social grace allows individuals to flexibly adjust their approach, ensuring that they can engage comfortably with a wide range of people.

9. Enhancing Professional Relationships:

In the context of business and professional relationships, social grace is vital for building strong networks, fostering collaborations, and making a positive impact.   Effective causal conversation with social grace can lead to new opportunities, partnerships, and a stellar professional reputation.

10. Personal Growth and Development:

Finally, embracing social grace in causal conversation is not just about external interactions; it also contributes to personal growth and development. It cultivates qualities like empathy, active listening, and effective communication, which can benefit individuals in all areas of life.

IMPORTANCE OF CAUSAL CONVERSATIONS TO A NEW BUSINESS

Causal conversation might seem inconsequential in the world of business, where serious discussions about products, services, and strategies often take center stage. Causal conversation is not just idle conversation; it's a powerful tool for relationship building, networking, problem-solving, and establishing your business's presence in the industry. By recognizing the importance of small talk and honing your skills, you can leverage its potential to benefit your new business in numerous ways, ultimately contributing to your company's growth and success.

However, it's important to recognize that small talk plays a crucial role in building and sustaining a successful business. Here's an extensive look at how causal conversation can be of great importance to a new business:

1. Relationship Building:

Causal conversation is the foundation of relationship building in the business world. Before diving into complex negotiations or transactions, people often engage in light conversation to establish rapport and trust. This initial rapport can pave the way for more meaningful interactions and partnerships.

2. Networking:

For a new business, networking is often a lifeline. Causal conversation is an essential networking tool. It allows you to connect with potential clients, partners, investors, and collaborators. Networking through small talk helps you expand your professional circle and discover new opportunities for growth.

3. Breaking the Ice:

When you're entering a new industry or market, causal conversation can break the ice in unfamiliar territory. It provides a comfortable entry point to engage with industry veterans, competitors, and potential clients. By engaging in small talk, you can gather valuable insights and establish a presence within your industry.

4. Market Research:

Conversations that start as causal conversation can quickly evolve into opportunities for market research. By asking the right questions and listening actively, you can uncover pain points, industry trends, and customer preferences that inform your business strategy.

5. Building Trust:

Causal conversation allows you to showcase your personality and character. It's an opportunity to demonstrate your professionalism, reliability, and authenticity. When people feel comfortable with you on a personal level, they are more likely to trust you in business dealings.

6. Employee Engagement:

For a new business, keeping employees motivated and engaged is essential. Engaging in small talk with your team members can create a positive workplace culture. It helps you understand their concerns, build camaraderie, and foster a sense of belonging within your organization.

7. Problem Solving:

Effective problem-solving often begins with a casual conversation. When you engage in small talk with colleagues or employees, you may discover issues or challenges that need addressing. Small talk can be a forum for brainstorming solutions and seeking input from various perspectives.

8. Conflict Resolution:

Causal conversation can also be a valuable tool for resolving conflicts within the workplace. Engaging in non-confrontational conversations allows you to address issues calmly and find common ground. It can defuse tension and lead to more productive outcomes.

9. Marketing and Sales:

Causal conversation can be instrumental in marketing and sales efforts. Whether it's at a trade show, conference, or social event, casual conversations can generate leads, create brand awareness, and promote your products or services indirectly. It can also provide valuable feedback on customer needs and preferences.

10.Company Culture:

The culture of your business is vital to its long-term success. Causal conversation contributes to creating a positive company culture by fostering open communication, collaboration, and a friendly atmosphere. When employees feel comfortable engaging in small talk, they are more likely to communicate effectively and contribute to a vibrant work environment.

11.Building a Brand Personality:

Small talk can help shape your brand's personality. It's an opportunity to convey your company's values, mission, and culture. By consistently engaging in positive and meaningful small talk interactions, you can reinforce your brand's identity and reputation.

12.Crisis Management:

In times of crisis or change, small talk can help leaders connect with employees, clients, and stakeholders on a personal level. It allows you to convey empathy, provide reassurance, and maintain transparency during challenging periods.

IMPORTANCE OF CAUSAL CONVERSATIONS TO ALREADY ESTABLISHED BUSINESS

Causal conversation remains relevant and essential for already established businesses, just as it is for new ones. In fact, small talk continues to play a significant role in maintaining and furthering an established business's success.

Causal conversation remains a powerful tool for established businesses in fostering employee engagement, maintaining a positive company culture, building strong relationships with employees and customers, and staying adaptable and competitive in a dynamic market. By recognizing the importance of small talk and nurturing it as a valuable skill within the organization, established businesses can continue to thrive and evolve in an ever-changing business landscape.

Here's an in-depth exploration of how small talk can be of importance to an already established business:

1. Employee Engagement and Retention:

In established businesses, maintaining a motivated and engaged workforce is crucial. Causal conversation with employees fosters a sense of belonging, trust, and camaraderie. When employees feel valued and connected on a personal level, they are more likely to remain loyal to the company, leading to lower turnover rates and reduced recruitment costs.

2. Team Building:

Causal conversation can be instrumental in team building efforts. Whether during team meetings, casual lunches, or social events, it helps employees get to know each other on a personal level. This, in turn, enhances teamwork, collaboration, and communication within the organization.

3. Leadership and Management:

For leaders and managers within an established business, small talk provides an opportunity to connect with team members and direct reports. These informal conversations can build trust, offer insights into employee concerns, and create a more supportive work environment.

4. Innovation and Problem Solving:

Small talk often leads to informal brainstorming sessions, where employees may share innovative ideas or suggest solutions to existing challenges. Encouraging such conversations can spark creativity and drive problem-solving efforts within the company.

5. Customer Relationships:

In the business world, strong customer relationships are paramount. Small talk is an effective way for sales and customer service teams to build rapport with clients. By engaging in personal conversations and showing genuine interest in customers' needs and experiences, businesses can strengthen customer loyalty and satisfaction.

6. Networking and Partnerships:

Even established businesses continue to expand their networks and seek opportunities for growth. Small talk at industry conferences, trade shows, and networking events helps businesses establish new partnerships, explore potential collaborations, and stay updated on industry trends and market changes.

7. Employee Wellness and Mental Health:

The well-being of employees is a growing concern for businesses. Small talk can serve as a means to check in on employees' mental health and overall well-being. This can help identify and address stressors or concerns early, promoting a healthier and more productive workforce.

8. Crisis Communication:

During times of crisis or change, small talk can play a vital role in internal and external communication. Leaders can use casual conversations to convey transparency, empathy, and reassurance to employees, clients, and stakeholders, helping to manage crisis situations more effectively.

9. Company Culture Maintenance:

Small talk contributes to maintaining and reinforcing a positive company culture. It keeps employees connected to the company's values and mission, even as the business grows. A strong company culture helps guide decision-making, attract top talent, and maintain a cohesive organization.

10. Market Research and Customer Feedback:

Small talk can provide valuable insights into market trends, customer preferences, and competitors' activities. Engaging in conversations with customers, industry peers, and suppliers can yield useful information that helps the business adapt and remain competitive.

11. Sales and Marketing Insights:

In established businesses, sales and marketing teams can gain valuable insights from small talk interactions. These insights can inform marketing campaigns, product development, and sales strategies. Understanding customer pain points and needs through informal conversations can lead to tailored solutions and improved customer satisfaction.

12. Community Engagement and Corporate Responsibility:

Established businesses often seek ways to give back to the community and demonstrate corporate responsibility. Small talk can facilitate connections with community organizations, allowing businesses to identify meaningful opportunities for social impact and philanthropy.

CONCLUSION

As we reach the final pages of "Talk Your Way to Success: Unveiling the Secrets of Effective Communication" we find ourselves at the intersection of knowledge and action, where theory transforms into practice and insights become the catalyst for change.

Throughout this journey, we have explored the profound significance of social grace in the context of business growth. We've learned that beneath the surface of everyday conversations lies the potential to forge powerful connections, stimulate innovation, and elevate your professional endeavors to new heights.

But knowledge alone is not enough; it is in the application of this wisdom that true transformation occurs. The pages of this book have provided you with a wealth of strategies, techniques, and principles to integrate into your daily interactions. From the art of the graceful introduction to the subtleties of active listening, you now possess a toolkit to navigate the intricate world of business relationships with confidence and poise.

Yet, mastering social grace is not solely about personal gain. It's also about giving back to your professional ecosystem. As you cultivate meaningful connections and elevate those around you, you contribute to a culture of collaboration, trust, and reciprocity. In doing so, you become a catalyst for positive change not only within your own business but also within your industry and community.

In closing, remember that the journey of mastering social grace is ongoing. Like any skill, it requires dedication, practice, and a commitment to continual growth. As you embark on this path, embrace each interaction as an opportunity to learn, connect, and leave a lasting positive impression.

As you put these principles into practice, watch as your business flourishes, your network expands, and your impact deepens. And in those moments of reflection, when you consider the distance you've traveled from the moment you opened this book to now, may you recognize the profound transformation that effective causal communication has brought to your professional life.

So, dear reader, I encourage you to step forward with newfound confidence, armed with the knowledge that social grace and the power of effective causal communication is not merely a skill but a force capable of propelling your business toward unprecedented success. Use it wisely, use it generously, and use it to forge the meaningful connections that will shape your future and leave an indelible mark on the world of business.